Selling to Restaurants: How to Sell, Service and Negotiate With Chefs and Restaurant Owners

Category:	Business & Economics
Author:	Bob Oros
Publisher:	Bob Oros Books
Copyright Year:	© 2019
License:	Standard Copyright License
ISBN	978-0-359-96227-3

Description: If you are one of the thousands of sales professionals, brokers, manufacturers, restaurant owners and/or chefs, this book was written for you. You will learn step by step how to build better relationships and negotiate win/win contracts with every customer or vendor resulting in increased sales starting immediately. You will also learn how to improve in the areas of food cost, labor cost, menu pricing, as well as tips on how to sell beef, pork, poultry and seafood.

Keywords: foodservice sales, broker sales, distributor sales, food manufacturer sales, selling to restaurants, selling to chefs, restaurant owner's resource

ISBN 978-0-359-96227-3

About the author, Bob Oros

After serving 6 years in the US Navy, Bob went to work in the food industry. He started by completing a three-year program to become a Certified Meat Cutter. He has personally processed everything from a 200-pound sea turtle to a 1,000-pound moose. Moving on, he worked as a sales manager and general manager for a meat processing company, a sales manager and general manager for a 50 million dollar per year distribution company, and an independent food broker covering the state of Florida. He eventually joined a Fortune 200 food company as their regional manager and within 2 years was promoted to national sales manager. The company had 80 salespeople and sold worldwide through 100+ brokers.

Bob Oros became a full-time speaker and author in 1992. He has presented over 2,000 sales training seminars in all 50 states and several international locations. Bob has trained more salespeople than any other person in the history of the foodservice industry. He is also the author of 60+ books on sales and marketing (Google: Bob Oros Books).

CSP Award: Bob Oros was awarded the designation of Certified Speaking Professional (CSP) by the National Speakers Association and the International Federation for Professional Speakers. Fewer than 10% of all speakers worldwide can qualify.

PWA Member: As a member of the Professional Writers Alliance along with his 35 years of B2B sales experience, Bob writes sales letters and training programs that will have you leaning forward asking for more.

I am the only person in the world who holds the two professional designations of CMC, certified meat cutter, and CSP, certified speaking professional.

A unique combination that will make a great presenter for your next meeting or special event.

www.BobOros.com | Bob@BobOros.com

Table of Contents

Chapter 1 - Attitude

Staying positive

The foodservice industry is a fast-paced business with continuous challenges, opportunities and problems to solve. A great day starts with a great attitude. If you wake up and immediately are in a bad mood, it isn't going to get any better. If you wake up grateful for another opportunity to make a difference, I can guarantee you are in for a real treat. Nobody wants to be around someone who is constantly negative. How can you grow as an individual when that's all you feed yourself? Staying positive in a world full of negatives will certainly make you stand out from the rest.

Your most important sale

The most important sale to make is the one you make to yourself. It will be very difficult to sell anything to a customer when you don't believe in yourself or the product you're selling. Setting goals will always keep you motivated and striving towards something that has meaning to your life. When you keep your eye on the reward, it's hard to not stay motivated and striving towards the personal satisfaction you will get from achieving what you have set out for yourself.

Apply what you learn

You can listen to all the sales seminars, read motivational quotes, read books, listen to audios, but at the end of the day, if you aren't willing to get out there and try, you're only cheating yourself. Experience will come with time, and with that experience will bring valuable lessons. It is our job each and every day to use the knowledge we learned the day before, apply it to today and try and make today better than yesterday.

Confidence takes time

Confidence in sales does take a while. No matter how good you feel about yourself, this industry can beat you down in a heartbeat. What makes it an interesting ride is when you pick yourself up after each time you get knocked down. It took me years to build the confidence and knowledge of the products that I was selling. The good part is, you don't have to know all the answers. Sometimes the best answer is' "I don't know, but I will get you that information right away." And follow up like a professional.

Be a problem solver

The best approach to problems is to always to be part of the solution. We talked about the confidence you have in yourself, but another important lesson is the confidence that your customer has in you. You have to make them feel like you're working with them, but really, you're also working for them. We can talk about price all day and sometimes yours might not beat the competition, but your service will. You will build confidence in knowing that "when you buy from my company, you get me along with it."

Reapply what you learn

Another important lesson is having the will to never quit. To have the attitude that nothing is going to stand in the way of reaching your goals. To take a lesson from every situation that happens and see it as a positive or a negative, apply it next time, and reapply it again and again. If you keep doing this, you will have what it takes to succeed in not only sales, but to succeed in life itself.

Credibility

Accountability for every circumstance, good or bad, is how you build credibility. To hold yourself accountable on the promises you make will go a long way with your customer. It is your job to make the customer feel like he/she is the single most important thing, and they really are. They are helping you support a family, buy your home, get that new car, etc. The customer has the power to decide who they want to buy from, and trust is a huge determining factor in the role of credibility.

Set yourself apart

The best way to separate yourself from the competition is to know everything about not only your products or services, but by knowing how your products or services can make a positive impact on your customer. There has to be a benefit to the customer in order for them to feel like you are trying to add to the success of what they are already doing. This speaks in volumes because as salespeople, we have to continuously learn new things, and then go out and apply what we have learned so that we can become a bank of knowledge for the customer.

Build personal relationships

The best way to build personal relationships is by being the absolute best version of "you" every day. Attitude is what makes or breaks a person in every area of life. If the day starts off with a terrible attitude, you're in for a long day; likewise, if your day starts off with a positive attitude then no matter what gets thrown your way throughout the day you will be able to adapt to certain situations and always keep your spirits high. No one wants to be around a negative person, even when times are good. Helping others is an important goal, and in business this should be constant. We have to always be concentrated on the customer and the tools we have to help them succeed.

Appreciate your customers

You MUST start your day with a great attitude, being thankful to wake up and able to help someone throughout your day. If we can live a life of service to others and appreciation for all the things in it, this will certainly spill over into your business. A simple THANK YOU can go a long way with your customer and help grow a relationship that will be permanent. In doing so you will not only beat the competition, but you will keep your customers loyal to you.

Be a great listener

One of the important keys to selling is to be a great listener. Sales people often have this idea that they are the ones who should do all the talking. The truth is, a great salesperson is a great listener. Listen to their problems and come up with a solution that helps them.

The industry's definition of selling

The industry's definition of selling is service. This definition is so new it is not even in the dictionary or thesaurus. The dictionary says selling means to persuade, or influence on a course of action. The thesaurus says selling is "barter, exchange, trade, traffic, and vend. Nowhere does it say selling is SERVICE. Nowhere does it say selling is helping your customers become more successful and make more money. Serving your customer in a way that they feel you have their back 100% and whatever it takes to help them be successful is what will create lasting relationships in this business!

Handling rejection

Rejection in sales comes every day. Once again, the key is to have a great attitude. What knocks you down only makes you stronger. If your mindset is to be successful, this should be the driving factor in not letting rejection make you fail. Have the faith that things will manifest in every area of your life, the heart to never quit, and the drive to want to be better in every situation. With these skills, a simple NO can be used as a challenge. NO doesn't mean never; it simply means it is not the right time. Take the rejection to mean; I will see you next week. Persistence in sales wins the race!

The key to persistence

Resistance from customers comes every day. We live in an economy that is extremely price conscious and this can hurt your business if your price isn't lower than your competition. If we were to give up every time the competition beats our price, we would have a long road ahead of us. We, as salespeople, have to have the persistence to never quit and always looking for the next best opportunity to help our customers succeed.

Asking vs. telling

The single best approach to going after a new customer is to go in the account and ask questions. Get as much information from the prospect as possible so you can go back and research where you can be of value. A person who sees value in what you are selling is how to get new business, but a person who sees value in you fixing what they feel is broken is how you create lasting relationships. Do not go into a new account and give them all the information about your product right away, it will probably end up in the trash. But when you strategically target areas of where there is a need, then you have a person's interest.

Setting goals

Goals in life are one of the single most important facets of successful people. If we do not set goals for our life and career, we will just be taking up space and our life would seem to have no meaning. Although you may be getting your work done, without goals you will never amount to something great and your attitude will just be mediocre. But by setting goals for our lives, it gives us something to reach for, something to look after, and also will give us a sense of honor when those goals are pursued and reached.

Points of difference

Our goals in business should always be that of service.

Selling is all about helping each other make the best decisions and working towards something that is greater than the current level. It doesn't matter what profession you are in, helping each other become better than yesterday is the ultimate goal for anyone. Listen when all else fails, and you will have a better sense of what the customer wants. This way you will have actionable information to help them make the best decisions. At the end of the day, the product or service you are selling has very little to do with their decision to buy from you. But the **service** you offer with your products will be the determining factor in these situations.

Sense of urgency

Having a sense of urgency is a vital part in not only sales, but almost every aspect of your life. A sense of urgency is a skill that is developed over time by practice. A customer will feel like you have their back and you are there to serve them if they feel like you care. Returning phone calls promptly, getting answers for them when they need them, and always trying to better their business by serving them. This is the true sign of a professional when you have a sense of urgency to be of service.

UPOD

Under Promise Over Deliver. When the customer thinks that something is going to be done later than when it actually gets done shows a great sense of service to them and it goes a long way in building you relationship!

Sincerely care about customers

Always try to live your life by helping others. That is the true sign of any professional, the life of service. People will care about you, but first you must care about them. Be the type of person successful people want to be around. Your attitude shapes your day but also shapes the day of the customers that you are seeing. Having a specific benefit when talking to your customers will give them the tools they need to make the best decisions for their company. Put in the work and make it appealing to them to where they can't say no, because it makes so much sense to do business with you. Serve them as you would like to be served.

Overcome insecurity

One of the hardest feelings to overcome is the feeling of insecurity. We are always misguided by thinking of being rejected. The fear of failure should excite us instead of making us insecure. Failure should teach us valuable lessons so we can make better decisions in the future. If we don't fail at things in life, we won't be able to learn anything in the process. You get out what you expect. If you are always thinking you don't amount to anything, or you will never be successful, you WON'T be! On the other hand, if you expect to win, or be the best at what you do, even if reality doesn't seem like you are, your expectations should always be greater than your reality. Expect it to happen, and you will see your efforts start to become reality.

Take the risk out of selling

When you can adopt a sense of a "Never Die' attitude, you can easily take the risk out of selling. Waking up every morning and being able to get another chance to make a difference should be your motivation. We all know that the more calls or presentations we make, the greater the return. Put in the work like you know you are supposed to and have goals to where you are reaching for something bigger than the present. You will fail but if you keep on going and keep moving forward, it is inevitable that your sales will come, and the business will increase. There should be no fear of failure because the next possibility for a sale is right around the corner.

Expectations and selling

Expectations have everything to do with the sale. If you try to sell something to someone but you expect them to say no, you just killed your delivery and your expectation will come off to whoever you're talking to. Try it another way; try delivering your product of service with the expectation that they won't have a choice to tell you no. If your approach is that of service and always trying to make things easier for your customer by the research you did before the call, they will see the meaning behind your efforts. The single most common thing about all successful people is that they all expect to WIN! It is an attitude that you must wake up every morning with. Make sure your goals and your expectations are in harmony with each other and worked towards in the most positive way possible.

Review your success

Success is a very important aspect of everyone's life. It gives us a sense of self-worth and pride in doing our daily activities. In life, there will also be failures and times that we try but we just weren't able to reach our goal. It happens all the time and there is nothing we can do about being knocked down. Reviewing all areas of your life, including your success can only result in a better outcome the next time. Successful people build on their achievements and expect greater things each time they achieve a goal. If you are always expecting the same thing, there is no growth and growth in sales is imperative. After every call or situation, take some information from it that you thought you did right, and build on those aspects. This will lead to making sure that you set yourself up for success.

Chapter 2 - Negotiating Price

Add value to every product

Shopping prices is an everyday occurrence, especially in this industry and economy. A buyer is inclined to ask for a discount from every salesperson that calls on them. One way to overcome this objection is to create a relationship with your customer. Let them know that you are loyal to them and your goal is to add value and success to their company.

The best way to make buyers understand when a price is higher than the competition is to let them know that when buying my product, they are also buying me. I will go to bat for them day in and day out. Whether that means dealing with issues that happen, finding better ways to better their business, or even just as simple as a "thank you".

Every company has overhead, and if you lower your price further than what your overhead calls for, you are doing more harm than good. No one works for free and lowering your price too much, hurts more than you may realize.

Never cut your price without being asked

We as salespeople should never make ti so easy to reduce our price. Know your product and all the benefits of what you are trying to help the buyer with. Consider what you are selling is a BENEFIT and anything that can benefit a buyer should also attach some worth to the product. Have confidence when presenting and be stern as to why your product is priced the way it is. Go over all the benefits with the idea why your product is priced where it is. The benefits should shine brighter than reducing your price. Reducing your price too quickly says that there could possibly already be a markup, that your product really isn't what you say it is, and so many other opinions if you are too quick to lower your price before they understand the benefits of it.

Make yourself more trustworthy

Selling is a very difficult industry, no matter what people try to tell you. It takes guts to go out on a limb and try to convince someone that they should buy your products or services.

Some salespeople take advantage of customers by exaggerating what they are selling.   This will ruin a relationship they could have spent years trying to create. A sales pitch or presentation should always be backed up by intelligence on how you can benefit the customer and their success. Helping buyers understand the importance of buying from you is solely your responsibility as a salesperson. How will your product benefit the customer, and then back it up by facts? This process will create a level of trust with your customer that will make it hard for them to turn to anyone else for advice.

Letting your customer know that you have done your research, and that you have what it takes to save them on labor costs, increase sales, or increase profits by using your products is ultimately the best way to create lasting relationships in business.

Shocked at your price

It is a buyer's job to make you feel like you are out of your mind when presenting your price. It is a tactic that is seen every day when selling. As salespeople and professionals, it is our job to not let this facial expression of shock get to us but reverting back to making them understand why your price is what it is. The benefit of buying from you and the benefit of using your product is exactly what will justify your price.

The fact that you are working for them, the benefit of them knowing you will answer when they call, the trust they have in you when issues arise, are all benefits of justifying your price.

Helping people understand that price is more than just monetary value will help you when selling something that is more expensive than your competition. Sometimes it is the yield of the product, quality, service, etc. These are all facts of why your product is rated the way it is.

The higher authority strategy

It is our responsibility to pitch our products and services to the people who are making the decisions. You don't want to go into a meeting with a customer who does not have the final say.

When faced with a potential prospect, start the conversation by saying, "If I have a product that can benefit your business, would you be the person to make the final decision to buy from me?" This will give you the ability to qualify potential clients and get appointments with the higher authority people.

Always ask for the name of the person that makes the decisions. This way you can set appointments with all of those people before going into a meeting.

Go into a kitchen and talk to everyone, introduce yourself to everyone including the dish washer. This is a great strategy because even if you don't set off the right vibe to the decision maker, you did to someone else within the company. When the buyer is making decisions, they sometimes get help from the people who responded favorable the moment you walk in. Sometimes these same people can make a buyer rethink why buying from you would be beneficial to their success.

The good guy – bad guy strategy

Good guy/Bad guy strategies are used every day, sometimes not even knowing they are being used. Don't get alarmed when you think you are becoming victim to it. Instead ask for clarity, call their bluff, and make them understand exactly what they are doing.

A great tactic is letting them know you are aware of what they are trying to accomplish. Use the tactic right back at them and if you're being the good guy, bring in a bad guy of your own and watch how fast their tactics get diminished.

Is that the best you can do?

When faced with the question "Is that the best you can do" it is our job to turn the objection back on the buyer. Explain why the price of your products is justified, how you are also buying "me" along with the product.

Often times the customer/buyer will also continue to ask for a discount and then you can revert to your tactics previously learned, turning to your higher authority, playing the role of the bad guy, and if this still doesn't work, make it seem like you are really doing everything you can to get them the best deal you possibly can.

By immediately lowering your price, you are also lowering your credibility as well.

Overcome every objection

When dealing with any situation where you must overcome objections, you want to have sympathy and a sense of understanding for the customers concern.

A great strategy is using the feel/felt/found approach to every situation. When faced with objections, having a sense of knowing how the customer feels will ultimately build the trust and make them feel as if you know exactly how they feel. Being able to overturn this tactic by simply understanding what they are doing. "I understand exactly what you are saying, my previous customer felt the same exact way, but when we sat down and actually looked at the facts, we found that by doing it this way they were able to save money off their overhead, create more sales, add profits, etc."

This will again, build the trust that you need to have a lasting relationship and a buyer who puts their faith in you and sincerely knows you are working for them and not just trying to get a sale.

Always ask why

In buying or selling, sometimes the best answer is to not have the answer. You never want to come across to any buyer and act like you have all the answers. When using this technique, most of the time you can get more information from the person you're talking to by asking more questions rather than feeding too much information. You always want to know about your products but being over knowledgeable can sometimes be a deal killer. Not knowing an answer to something can create a more lasting relationship by getting the answers to the questions that your buyer needs, and actually following up when you say what you are going to do.

Never make the first offer

It is a buyer's job to ask for the best possible price. Lowering your price too quickly can make it seem like price can be lowered on every item they ask for. Having the knowledge of what your buyer is paying or the price that they need to be, can make it much easier to sell something at the price that matches what they are looking for. This can also add to your gross profits as well if you know what they are paying and coming in at a price that is just slightly lower than what they are paying versus a price that is much lower than what they are paying.

Don't imply too much flexibility

Stating your price to any buyer should always be a firm answer. The statement "somewhere around" can easily give the flexibility of the price and the buyer knows exactly what to do when this happens. This automatically lets the buyer know there is some flexibility in the price, and it is their job to get you down as low as they possibly can. Practicing delivering your price with confidence makes it seem like what you are selling is very important and the price is reflective of the quality of the product or service in question.

Add on sales

When a buyer agrees to your price too quickly, 9 times out of 10 there will be some sort of add on statement that soon follows. Once you have agreed on your sale, there is a natural tendency to leave as fast as you can. Knowing that this was too easy, you subconsciously know that there will be some sort of terms that are required and normally it happens as soon as the agreement to purchase something is over. By getting a commitment first, it makes it easier for the buyer to justify the decision and ask for add on orders.

Ask for something in return

Do not keep lowering your price or giving in to special requests too easily without asking for something in return. This is a very important strategy when dealing with buyers. Giving and taking are part of selling and they should not be taking as a sign of weakness. It is our job to offer the best we have to a customer, but it is also their job to offer the best they have in turn. We, as sellers, cannot assume the customer knows what we want. We have to make our requests loud and clear. Whenever we give in to a price reduction or a special request from a buyer, always ask for something in return.

The bait and switch

Bait and switch is an unfair practice and it is also against the law but still it happens all the time. A good salesperson may try and persuade you to buy a product or service that is higher quality or a different brand with more features at a higher price. This is a strategy used by very good salespeople, but what's important is that they are giving you the choice. You always want to keep in mind that if something sounds too good to be true, most of the time it is because of this very fact, IT IS! Always ask questions and make sure there is no underlying terms that can come back and bite you.

Never split the difference

We as salespeople should always be reluctant to give in to things too quickly. Every penny adds up to a lot of money over time and sometimes one dollar on a multi-case order can add to the profit and be a very large difference. Agreeing to split the difference too quickly can cost you a lot of money in some cases. We as sellers should always let the buyer offer to be the one to split the difference first. We should hear what they have to offer, and then make our next move. In practicing this technique, we can sometimes add more profit to our sale by not agreeing to quickly.

How people decide

Everybody who makes an important decision always wants to feel comfortable about making that decision. Making the buyer feel as comfortable and important as possible will create the impression that will last with whomever it is, you're pitching to. Making a customer feel safe about buying from you and making sure they know you have their back is ultimately how you create lasting relationships in business. No one ever wants to buy from someone who doesn't believe in their own products or services, so it is your job to make sure that your customers know that when they are buying from you, they are buying more than just your product or services.

How to control the interview

Preparation is the key to success in just about anything you do. You must be prepared when entering an interview and to take it a step further, you should always know what you would like to discuss. Buyers use a guide when ordering what they need, and it should be no different for us in sales. Having a guide with highlighted points that you would like to discuss will leave the impression that you mean business and understand the magnitude of what you are trying to discover for the customer.

Don't try to impress

When a person is trying to sell a product or service, the smartest thing you can do is notice something about the person you are trying to sell to and make them aware of how impressed you are with what you see. Everyone loves a good compliment, and everyone hates someone trying to sell something to them. To create lasting relationships in business you must have a sense that everyone is human and that everyone has feelings just like you.

The best way to impress your customers, is to tell them how much you appreciate what they do or find something you have in common. A customer will relate to you if indeed you take the time to notice that you have common interests, likes, dislikes, family background, etc.

Ask for advice

The same common denominator is also here in this question. People like to feel important and that is just the bottom line. Everyone has a story; some might be going through something you have no clue about. When you sincerely ask for someone's advice, the attention of that person will immediately perk up and they will certainly feel important enough to offer what you ask. Customers like to feel important and if the vibe they get from you is just that, it is nearly impossible that they will not buy from you.

Getting someone's advice might also lead to new roads that you never expected or didn't think of in the way they put it. You don't always have to act on something someone tells you, but if you are faced with answers that make sense, it wouldn't hurt to try and see the outcome.

Justify rather than discount

It is the buyer's job to ask for a discount and 99% of the time you will get asked that question. It is our job to understand that justifying why our price is the way it is and making the customer understand that price isn't the only thing that he/she should be looking at. A customer must have trust in you that your product will be delivered as described, quality of the products plays an important role, your product may have less operational costs, labor costs, etc. These are all great attributed that will help justify your product's price and make it to where you do not have to offer a discount.

Getting customers to change

No one likes to change. People create routines within their lives and when those routines are broken or change occurs, many times it gets better before it can ever get worse. Especially if someone has been doing it wrong the whole time and finally got the process right, change can throw things out of line until a routine gets into place again. This is the way things will always be. Resistance is part of everyone's life and a person can resist an idea for a number of reasons.

One great way to get your customer to change is by building trust and doing your homework. Know their business and your direct objections for wanting their business. Adding to the success to any company and making the buyer understand how will create less resistance in having a customer acceptable to change. Working with them throughout the whole process and making sure you go above and beyond, not just selling your product and going through the motions.

The choice set up

Using the choice set up when presenting and closing the sale can be a very successful technique. Offering someone the choice of something they don't want and also something they never knew they wanted until you gave them the choice can have an immediate impact whether or not you actually close someone on the deal. You can also do this with two options that you both want and give them the choice for them to pick.

Either way they choose, you win in both scenarios and you are allowing the customer to have full control on which one they choose. Makes them feel engaged and that they are making the right decision based on the information at hand.

Chapter 3 - The Selling Process

New customer sales process

New business is the life of your business; it is the backbone. It is what will take your business to the next level and adds to your success. There are 5 steps that you need to take in any sales approach and if you follow these steps, it is a definite that you will grow your business to new heights and land more deals. You must sell yourself first before you sell your product. Next you need to sell your company and then you can sell your product. Lastly, you should present your pricing and the next step is getting the buyer to accept your offer and start the buying process. If you completed all of these steps and still do not get the sale, then the prospect just may not be the customer you are looking for. DO not give up, keep moving forward and eventually the business follows your work ethic.

The Importance of planning

Planning plays an important role in everything we do in sales and business. There are no exceptions. Seventy eight percent of all salespeople fail due to lack of planning. In the past the market was not nearly as saturated with competitors doing the same thing as what you are doing. Times have changed and planning plays an important role in getting a buyer to consider your products instead of the competition. Planning how you will present your product, how you will suggest something on their menu, or just planning on how you will approach a buyer are all good examples of how planning can make a huge difference in success or failure.

One skill successful salespeople use

Selling is unlike any other profession. It requires a lot of self-discipline and your organization has to be impeccable. Planning is key to being successful in this profession. A great tool to use is to make a list of things that you have to do tomorrow and number them in the order of importance. Things will come up each day that will throw you off your plan but having this list to come back to can help for you to continue to keep on your plan and stay on track.

How small companies get big

The topic of all conversations of a person who is trying to be most successful, is growth. How do you grow? Growth starts with a goal. Once the goal is recognized, it takes an immense amount of thinking, planning, and action towards reaching that goal. This should be the case for everything you do in business. In large companies you usually have a CEO which creates the plan and direction of the company and everyone knows who they are, what they want to become, and how they are going to get there. It is much different for small companies. Small companies need to create a presentation in hope to sell to potential shareholders/investors. Create a detailed plan on where you will be in one year, five years, and so on so that they too can see the vision of the company.

A born salesperson

There is no such thing as a "natural born" anything. To be great at something requires a vision, and then attacking that vision full force. Practice makes perfect and you have to trigger those skills daily so you can be at whatever it is you set out to be. Planning will give you the skills and qualities that you need to be successful in selling. Plan you next week, your next month, your next year and you will be surprised at the results. Make a commitment to yourself that you are going to be the best at what you do, and no matter how many times you fail, you will succeed. The information you learn from failures will be used in the next battle to help you succeed better than the last time. You develop the skills by actually using them and trying to see what works best for you and capitalize on those aspects of your techniques. Always plan your tomorrow the day before, and you will see your results.

Overcome telephone reluctance

The telephone should be used as a tool to become more cost effective. Time management, carefully prepared sales presentations, and making firm appointments for new accounts are all skills that need to be mastered in order to be the best at what you do. Efficiency is defined as the ability to do the greatest amount of work, with the least amount of effort, in the shortest amount of time. We have to always be thinking of an easier way to do our job better. The telephone is an old tool that works better if it is used. One of the best ways to overcome telephone call reluctance is to have all your calls grouped together and make them all at once. If someone turns you down, you can move right along to the next one without even thinking about the last call. Every call should be tailored into making firm appointments, not to sell something to them right away. Once you get those appointments set, then it is your job to zero in on your presentation and find the need of the customer.

The secret of being a consultant

There are many qualities you have to acquire in order to separate yourself from competitors, but the one skill that will make you excellent at consulting is the ability to listen. Many salespeople have a completely different idea. They think that in order to sell something they must talk about the product as much as they can, when in turn, your objective is to gather as much information from the buyer that you can and tailor your presentation to what their needs are and how you or your product can be a solution. Asking questions is the single most important thing you can do when trying to gather information about your customer? Listen to their responses and understand the needs to better assist what you are trying to accomplish.

Lost in the first 60 seconds

We are living in a world of "information overload" with all the information that is at our disposal on a daily basis. To get a customer to listen, there is one of two things we can do. We can fall in with their attitude, or we can change it. In talking to anyone, whether selling a product or service or just chatting with someone on the street, the single best approach to use is to first get their attention. Ninety percent of all sales are lost in the first 60 seconds. We automatically start off talking and forget that these are people who have problems just like you. In order to make them feel comfortable and show interest, you must first let them know you care, and you have their back. Ask question, ask for advice, make them respond and interact with the process.

When to stop talking

It is the idea that the salesperson should do all the talking, when in actuality it is just the opposite. Listening is a trait of a great salesperson because you have to find the need of the customer in order to help them make a better decision. You won't hear that need when you talk too much and don't listen. You must recognize the signs of a buyer when the right time is to close. Asking questions as to when they would like the product delivered, how many quantities they would like on their first order, etc. Get them talking about what they prefer and then capitalize on the statements of the buyer. Given that you can come through with all that was requested, it makes for an easy decision to buy from you.

How to design a presentation

Six questions you should ask when designing your presentation:

1. Do you have a price advantage or a price problem?
Whether or not your product or service has an advantageous price, make sure your benefits are strong enough to get people interested enough that price isn't necessarily what they are looking at.

2. Who is the person who will buy your product or service? You want to make sure you are presenting your product or service to the most influential person in the sale.

3. What are the economic benefits of using your product? You want to base your presentation off of your product having an advantage. How it can save your customer money, time, effort, etc. then you have an advantage over the competition.

4. What is the product made of or what does it consist of? Make sure you know every detail about the product of service you are selling.

5. What does your product or service do best? You must determine how or what will benefit the customer the best about your product or service.

6. How important are your competitive differences? Competitive advantages are great in a sale, but you have to keep in mind that you never want to knock the competition. Instead, we need to make sure we explain the difference between the two and always compare apples to apples.

Making a first impression

The first minute of any presentation is the most important than any other step in the process. You have to grab the attention of the customer within the first minute and make it seem appealing to why they should be listening to what you have to say. It is more than likely that you have 3 seconds to get their attention, and then 30 seconds to tell your story. You must first get their attention, and this will spark their interest. Once the interest is obtained you can continue to spill out the details as to why you are presenting and what it is you are trying to accomplish. Once all of these have been strategically handled, it is time for action and ready for the close. Attitude is the most important aspect of this entire process and you should know that in order to grab someone's attention and being able to even start to present, you must have the most positive attitude of anyone in the room. I can promise you it will rub off on even the most negative person in the room.

Prepare them for your presentation

Your first words in any presentation should grasp the attention of whom you are presenting. You should prepare your prospect for what they are about to learn. Your presentation should be used in terms of a good teaching job. Do not just show how your product is used or what it is made of. They need to see the advantages of how it can add to their success by using it. You should always prepare your presentation around the importance of the goals of the prospect and tailoring your presentation around this simple fact. People want to hear about the advantage of using your product over another, or how using your product or service can help their future be a little easier and more profitable.

Focus on their future

Politicians do not talk about their needs, yet they always are talking about the future and what they will do to better life in the future. They know that to be successful and stay in office they have to give the people what they want and make it a part of every speech that they give. Insurance companies are no different, they also talk about the future. The future full of accidents, fires, floods, natural disasters, all of which makes you think that you will need this service in case one day in the future you will need it. Selling is also no different. People want to hear how your product of service will add to the success of their future. People should have long term goals and if anything can add to those goals for the future, you will have their attention immediately and make sure that what you are selling has some importance to their future as well.

Put customers on a magic carpet

This topic is a key to a highly successful salesperson. The average salesperson talks about price or the competition, but always in the present tense. The consultative salesperson looks at this in a different way and looks how it can benefit the future of the customer. What are their goals for the future and how can the product of service add to those goals? You must make the customer feel like you have their best interest in the palm of your hands and nothing

Make irresistible presentations

Most presentations are focused around the wrong thing because we believe that in order to sell something you have to find the needs of the customer and then base your presentation around those needs. Most customers don't "need" anything. What makes an irresistible presentation is when you find out what the customer "wants" and let them know you can help them get it. Making a presentation around how your products and services will help the business and life of a customer and add to the success of their future is really what grabs people's attention. Doing a little bit of homework and understanding how to apply this important factor will separate you from the rest.

A carefully planned pause

A planned pause can be used for a couple different occasions in the selling process. Using a pause gives you the opportunity to carefully review what information is at hand so you can make the best next move. Taking notes at a sales presentation is a helpful way to use a pause. When you write down statements that are confusing, it lets the buyer know that you are listening and gives you the opportunity to think about how to overcome the objection rather than letting your emotions take over and ruin the sale. Pausing gives off the impression that you aware of the task at hand, but not carefully overcoming objections can make or break the sale.

What do buyers want?

A buyer doesn't want a salesperson. They want someone to help them make a good decision which often brings the sale. Making decisions based off of what you think would benefit their business is what they are looking for in a salesperson. One thing a buyer doesn't like is a pushy salesperson. One of the quickest ways to damage a relationship with a customer is to apply to much pressure into buying from you. Sound educated and study your products so that you can know the benefits of using yours compared to the competition. Have your buyer's best interest at heart and never try and sell something that you don't believe in first. To be a great salesperson you need to back your presentations with proof so that the buyer feels comfortable making the decisions that you are steering him towards.

Suggestive selling

When selling to a customer, a great tool to use that is often overlooked is suggestive selling. When you suggest something to a customer you are pretty much stating that you have something that might add to the success of their company. Sometimes the buyer may overlook these certain items or services but when you suggest it to them, you are saying that you know that what you are suggesting will work. It gives the buyer a sense that you have their back in certain situations. Most customers appreciate having their attention diverted to new and interesting ideas so using this technique can add to the sale. Constantly making suggestions is like planting the seed, the more you make suggestions to your customer, the better the opportunity of up selling your products or services.

Create demand

The more demand for something of value, the more value it is to that certain product of service. When selling anything of importance, make it seem like the product of service you have is so worthy that it may not be for everyone. The more interest you spark when making your presentation, the more demand there will be for your items. Not everyone should qualify to having your time and efforts to trying to add to the success of their company, and there should be a selective importance on whom you want to offer your products or services to.

Insurance against failure

In a growing market there will always be a cheaper product, lower costs, etc. It is our job as salespeople to understand the concerns for a customer and make our products and services top priority. When presenting your products, if you are approached with your price is too high, ask questions to find out why it is too high. When you get the prospect to start talking about why it is too high, you will uncover some truths about why they think that it is too high. Focus your presentation on the difference of the products, not the price. Paying a little more for quality is an investment or insurance in knowing you have a great product that will add to the success of what you are doing. Always do what you say you are going to do, that will go a long way to your customer.

How to overcome objections

Objections are a part of selling (and life). We even give objections in our own head when making decisions about anything. You should always know how to handle objections when they come up. The best approach to objections it to thoroughly understand what the customer is objecting to and help them work through the issue. Taking responsibility for finding a solution will encourage the customer to work with you. You want to always have a great understanding that when doing business with you, you are the one that will work the hardest for your customer. You will advance into the next phase of your career when you make it no longer all about yourself.

Smoke screen objections

The best way to handle smoke screen objections is to agree with the objection, but you should also respond saying, "I am glad you brought that up!" This is the time to ask your question and find out why it is that the customer feels the way they do. Most of the time this will get the prospect to admit to himself that what he is objecting isn't valid at all. Asking questions about their objections creates the appearance that you do care about their concerns, but it will also get the customer talking about his/her objections and may answer their own arguments.

Avoid going on the defensive

Every customer has a job, and their first objective is to take control of the salesperson. But what happens when we try this process in reverse? It is true that no one can sell something to anyone that they do not want, it is impossible.

Selling is about helping people with your products and services being used to make better decisions for the customers. I like to think of my career in sales is ultimate job to help people, but not every prospect that I encounter will be the right person for my products or services. I get to pick who I want to do business with as well and when you take this approach in selling, your life gets a whole lot easier. Discovering the benefits as to why someone should buy from you rather than the competitor is imperative in the selling process. They MUST feel like buying from you is a better decision than buying from anyone else.

Deny or admit an objection

This is very simple, deny the objection when it is false, and admit the objection when it is true. Customers like honesty and this is a fact in all aspects and relationships in life. We can enter into a denial if the customer questions your own honesty and integrity or the same of your company. This is a type of denial that can be contested because what they are objecting, you know it to be completely and 100% false. On the other hand, some objections to buying cannot be overcome or denied, because you know these to be 100% true. In these cases, a great way to overturn these objections is by presenting the benefits of your products and services and make it known that you are there to help.

Buying on price

In today's economy, people will always be concerned with price because over the last couple decades, costs of things are doubled, and often tripled. But there will also be companies out there who base their business off of being the cheapest and their products being on the lower end of all spectrums. This is just a simple fact of the world we live in. The key is to know everything about your products and services that you are selling so that you will know all the ins and outs of what you are doing. Quality cost more, in anything that you buy. Something you can get a cheaper product and get away with it, but then sometimes that very thing may not last as long or vice versa. Know your business environment and always be on the lookout for points of interest and points of difference that will keep you having the competitive advantage over your market.

Closing the sale

A great salesperson is an assistant to the buyer. Without good salespeople, the customer will be lost when trying to make decisions. There are so many products coming on the market every day and so many choices that a buyer has to make. Our job is to make their life a little easier. Being a great salesperson requires you know when and how to close.

The direct close requires that you start your presentation by asking for what you want and then build your presentation around it.

The choice close is another common close and it requires you to build your presentations by offering two or more different choices and explaining features and benefits of each one, then allowing your customer to choose what works best for them.

Another closing strategy is the time advantage close. This particular close creates a sense of urgency during the presentation and will make the buyer feel like if they do not act now, they could be losing out.

Lastly, an effective closing strategy is the ask again close. Ask for the order, wait a short period of time and then ask again as if it were your first time. Anyone can ask once and accept the negative response, but it takes a good closer to ask again and again.

Customers expect you to close

When presenting your product or service, a good sales professional will know when to close. The buyer expects you to close and those expectations have a time frame. Failure to close allows the competition to follow up on your sales points and possibly get the business that you worked so hard for, simply because you didn't ask for the order;

however, the competition did. You have to put yourself in the mind of the buyer and make your points tailored around how it can help their business. Once all the facts are out and you have the buyer's interest, you should always ask for an order while the buyer is excited about the presentation. Have the idea that what you are showing them is a no-brainer and go to every presentation expecting the best, and guess what, the best will come!

The best time to close

A huge part in the closing process is the planning of all the other things leading up to the close. Closing should be the easiest part of the selling process because it is all the other work leading up to the close where you strategically started the process of selling; this is the part that takes a strategic plan and some homework on your part.

I said this before and I am going to say it again, when you are selling, you have to believe in what you do and what you are selling. If you believe in the product or service that you are offering and know that what you are trying to do is help the customer have a better product or service, the closing is easy. It is just like going to a nice restaurant and having a great meal, you will show up the next day and tell everyone about how good the meal was. Selling should be no different. When the product or service you have is so good, you want to tell everyone so that they can make a good decision for their future.

Appeal to their buying senses

Most customers want to see how your product or service can help them. They need to see with their own eyes and have a vision about how it will help their future and their business. Giving presentations that will be visual to see the effects of what you are trying to accomplish will go a long way in the sales process of your presentation. Keep your language simple, always assume he or she knows nothing about your product. You should always be enthusiastic about what you are selling. No one likes to even talk to a negative person so when you create a sense of positivity about what you are selling, the better your chances on closing on the sale.

Let the customer do the closing

When a customer has made up their mind that they are going to buy, they buy, and nothing is going to stop that process. One of the highest skills of any salesperson is getting the customer to see in their imagination how your products of service will be an advantage to their future. Ask questions, get the customer to talk and most of the time you will locate a need somewhere in their story. Wrap your closing around the need and tailor your entire presentation around the advantage and the needs of the customer. Once you can master this skill, the customer almost always closes themselves because they see the need of using your product or service.

How many customers

The average salesperson sells a little over 2 million dollars per year, or $40,000 per week. The average order size in the industry is $500. This equates to having 80 accounts buying $500 every week. But in all honesty that is really not a good plan. If we can strategically pick the customers that would double the size of our orders, that is ideally the customers you want. We shouldn't even worry about low margin customers and work on the ones that can give decent volume. Then you are making the correct decisions by basing your customer base on high volume, high margin orders. This will create a customer base that will exceed the average industry rate.

Selling with focus

Focus is another single most important aspect of selling, or really anything in life that will grant results. If you are not focused on the task at hand and what you are trying to accomplish, I can guarantee you that half of what you learned will be lost in the process of your daily activities. In order to increase your sales goals, you must focus in on where you can strategically make a difference. Show the qualities that you value in yourself and bring your best foot forth to each day, and sales will follow not far behind. It takes confidence in yourself, and a constant focus on your craft to be very successful in this business. Target the opportunities you have and focus on all the aspects to get to the closing, and growth is inevitable. Focus on how you will be of benefit to the customer; the solution to their needs!

How to you set your price

In any business, you must sell your product or service at a price that makes a profit. Your gross profit is based on your price, multiplied by your number of units of sale, minus your costs. Some customers base their decisions on buying on price alone, but that should not determine how you discount your product. Your price in most cases should be somewhere between your cost and your competitor's price.

What price tells your customers

Price is a very important element in the market strategy. Price can tell your customers a lot about your product or service strictly by how it is priced in the market. If your price is higher than most or the competitors, this can create a sense of a higher quality product. With intelligent pricing, you can outsell your competitor and get a bigger share of the market. Do not be so quick to discount your product, but instead, offer the advantages of why you have a higher price.

Set yourself apart

The first step of setting yourself apart from your competition is by making a commitment to yourself that this is what you want to do and you will not stop trying until you are the best at what you do. This simple fact can create an attitude that is unmatched when seeking new customers. When you promise a customer that you are going to do something for them, and actually following through with what you said you are going to do. Treating your customer exactly how you would want to be treated and understanding that they are people just like you, with needs and wants. To be able to handle their needs and wants and excel in helping them succeed. Pay close attention to all the details and making them know you have their back.

One good reason to buy

Every salesperson should have that "sizzle" about their sales efforts that it should make the customer feel like they need to buy from you. Once you get the good reason that they should buy from you, it should be part of every sale pitch or marketing effort. The more you focus on promoting yourself and being a professional, will create a sense that you are an expert at what you do.

How many calls

I never like to put an exact number on the calls you should be making only because I think we all know, that the more calls you are making, and the more appointments you set up to present your product or service, the better your closing ration will be. Sometimes selling your product or service just doesn't happen the first call, so it is very important that we strategically target the customers that we want to have in our book of business and do not let anything stop us from getting them as a customer. It could often take at least 10 calls and 10 separate visits in order to finally close a deal, but persistence usually wins the race!

Personal details

One of the most positive characteristics about a salesperson is the pride they have in knowing everything about their customer. This fact is very true and will create a long-lasting relationship and will give a sense that you care about what you are doing and what you are trying to accomplish FOR your customer. Anyone can sell something to someone, but it takes more information than that in order to keep that customer for life. You have to know every little detail about what drives them as customers and the help you give them to reach their personal goals is like a pot of gold in the selling process.

An attitude of confidence

Have you ever been around a negative person for so long that you start inheriting that negative spirit yourself? It is like a ball and chain that is holding you back from being the best you can be. This important fact is not only applied to selling, it is applied to all aspects of life. People react to emotions and respond to the attitudes of other people, so we have to make sure that day in and day out we display the best qualities of ourselves to everyday life so that we can be the best we can possibly be. Before going in to see a customer, or make that sales phone call, try to go in with the best spirits and the best attitude that you possibly can. It may make the difference for you in making or breaking the deal.

Control their attitude

How you communicate with your customers can have the greatest effect on the overall attitude of the both of you.

There are many different types of people in this world and sometimes it can be very difficult dealing with some of the attitudes out there, but if we make a conscious effort to be the best we can be and have the best attitude possible, it will inevitably rub off on our customers as well. Trust is a huge deal in the selling process, and it can be built by having the best attitude possible, telling the truth, following up on promises, and making the most out of each day. Sometimes all it takes is a simple hello, or a nice gesture to lift someone's spirits. We all have something that we are going through and staying positive throughout the process can help everyone's attitude towards what they are trying to accomplish in their life and workplace.

A metal picture of the sale

Everyone's mental vision of who they are and what they would like to become is the most crucial experience in one's self worth. Having a vision of what you are trying to accomplish will give you a goal to work towards and something measurable for you to make it all a reality. If you mental attitude it filled with nothing but negative thoughts about yourself, your goals and your visions will slip through your fingers for the rest of your life. On the other hand, if your metal picture has your goals lined out and your attitude matches that specific vision, you will be in for a real treat. Preparation is the key and you should take on all the details about how your day can turn out, and build your attitude around your case. Every day we should all wake up and be thankful to be alive, and to help people succeed; this is what life is all about. Your attitude will follow!

The value of personal questions

Personal questions can build a relationship faster than trying to sell something. People often attach who they are to things they love to do outside of the workplace. Their office is usually a great place to see who these people are without even saying a word to them. Attach yourself to their life and find out who they are and what they want to become, what their interests are and why they do what they do! People find other people interesting by what they have in common, not by how different they are from themselves. When we relate to their goals of life and the vision that they have, what makes them happy is something that is a great place to start when building a relationship with a customer. Often times you will weed out the people who you want to do business with and the people that you don't just by asking personal questions. If your goals and what you are trying to become do not align with the specific person you are trying to do business with, then why do business with them?

Do you believe in superstitions?

Superstitions are for the people who will not be as successful as they possibly can. How can you put a superstition to sleep for good? Go the extra step and see what kind of results you get from that extra call, that extra presentation, that extra step towards getting a sale. Keep moving forward no matter how many times you fail, pick yourself back up and try again... and again... and again... until you succeed in whatever task is at hand. Once that task is completed, move to the next one and always be conscious of your next move that is going to make the difference.

Chapter 4 - Lowering Food Cost

Food cost vs. cost of food.

The difference between food costs and the cost of food is sometimes misinterpreted. Food cost is very different than the actual "cost of food".

The cost of food is what we pay to the distributor and is determined by adding up the invoices.

Food cost is determined in a completely different way.

To determine the actual food cost, you follow this formula:

Beginning Inventory
+ Purchases
– Ending Inventory
= Food Cost

To find the food cost percent divide your food cost by the dollar amount of sales for the same period.

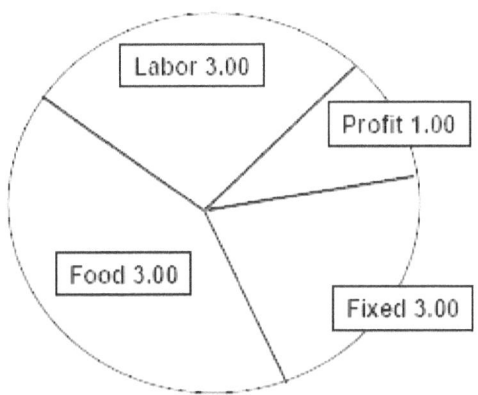

A profit and loss template

By using the 30 - 30 - 30 - 10 (Food cost 30%, Labor 30%, Fixed 30%, Profit 10%) as a template you can put together a P & L depending on what number you have for a month.

If you know their food cost is $9000:

$9000 divided by 30% = Sales should be $30,000.

Overhead should be $9000 and labor should be $9000

$9000 + $9000 + $9000 = $27000 leaving $3000 profit 10%

If you know their labor cost is $7500:

$7500 divided by 30% = Sales should be $25000

Overhead should be $7500 and food cost should be $7500

$7500 + $7500 + $7500 = $22500 leaving $2500 profit 10%

If you know their overhead cost is $18000:

$18000 divided by 30% = Sales should be $60,000

Food cost should be $18000 labor cost should be $18000

$18000 + $18000 + $18000 = $54000 / $6000 profit 10%

Finding discrepancies

When talking with operators and trying to help them add to the success of their company, we must take the approach of a consultant. Helping the operator understand all aspects of the food cost and how there are ways to cheat the system internally.

Back door policy

This is by far one of the most areas of concern in the food industry. The back door should always be locked and screened when people come through it. A lot of product walks out of the back door and operators don't even recognize until it's too late. If someone cannot seem to get a grasp on the ideal food cost, a good rule is to look at the back door and figure out if anything could be victim of theft.

Check invoices

Errors within invoices happen every day. Sometimes it could be an honest mistake when keying in the invoice. This factor can hurt food costs if you get overcharged for something within the invoice.

Checking in deliveries

If you buy it by the piece, Count it. If you buy it by the pound, Weigh it.

This happens all the time within the industry. Vendors know who does and who doesn't have a scale. For a customer who doesn't have a scale, it would be very easy to adjust the invoice to mark up a pound or two, and the customer would get charged for something he didn't get or use.

Nothing to do with price

The following have nothing to do with price but everything to do with food cost:

Portions size

Back door policy

Invoice mistakes

Checking in deliveries

Shrink and waste

Menu design and pricing

Over a period of time, with these discrepancies, it could seriously do some damage to the company in which these things are happening. We all need to understand the situations that can happen, and how we can better help operators understand all that could possibly take place to affect their numbers.

Actionable intelligence that can be used to figure out discrepancies can lead to a relationship where the operator relies on you and your skills to help them succeed.

Chapter 5 - Safely Handling Food

It costs the Federal Government millions of dollars a day to employ food inspectors to inspect the food we buy. Meat is the most tested and inspected food we buy. There are many different processes that should be adhered to so that we can ensure we are handling food properly and avoid making people sick.

The single most common issue that causes people to become sick from the food we purchase is Cross Contamination.

Cross contamination

Cross contamination occurs when bacteria from one thing gets on another thing from direct contact. Most of the time these cross contaminations can come from something as small as a knife or cutting board. Making sure we are handling things correctly and cleaning after each use can prevent someone from becoming very ill or even death.

The two basic sources of bacteria on beef are from the outside. Fur, feathers, scales, hair, and from the inside, meaning the digestive tract.

The source of bacteria on pork mainly come from the intestines. If there is a cut in the intestines, this can allow bacteria to escape and contaminate the meat.

The source of bacteria on poultry is very similar to pork in the fact of the intestines being the source of bacteria. The breakdown of poultry is mainly done by machines so this process has to be very carefully done.

The source of bacteria on seafood can happen by a number of ways. Making sure that seafood stays cold is a good way to make sure that the products stay fresh and the quality is up to standards. Sushi products should always be frozen first to kill bacteria if you are eating fish raw.

It costs an average of $74,000 to a foodservice operator for making someone sick. Bacteria is most commonly found on the surface of the meat. These particular bacteria can easily be transported by a person hands or tools. We must make sure that we keep a clean working station and make sure that we are handling everything with the most care and always try and make sure that we are never overlooking this safety processed.

Getting someone ill can cost someone a lot of money and in many cases can cause your operations to be closed down.

What you should know

In rare roast beef the internal temperature of the meat must be held at 135 degrees for no less than 35 minutes to kill bacteria.

If the internal temperature goes up to 150 degrees, the bacteria will be killed in one minute and at 165 degrees it will be killed in about 10 seconds.

Rare meat is safe as long as it is cooked and handled correctly.

When products are kept below 35 degrees bacterial growth will virtually stop.

It is important to remember that most bacteria are not damaged or killed by freezing, they simply do not multiply.

Bacteria will grow and multiply at temperatures between 40 and 140 degrees with the most rapid growth in the temperature range of 80-100 degrees.

Thawing should always be done in the refrigerator or under cold running water to prevent rapid growth of surface bacteria.

If you cut up a fresh chicken on a cutting board and then make a salad, without washing the knife and cutting board, surface bacteria can be transmitted to the salad.

Cross contamination can even occur by not properly washing hands after handling fresh meat or wiping hands on an apron before washing them. The apron then becomes a carrier of bacteria.

An example of a problem occurred when fresh chicken was cut, and the cutting board was not washed. Rare prime ribs were served, and everyone became sick with salmonella.

The bottom line of food safety

1. Treat all meat "As if" it was contaminated, and the surface likely contains salmonella and E coli.

2. Treat all food that is in the temperature zone of 40 to 140 "As if" surface bacteria is growing at a very rapid speed.

3. Assume that your hands, cutting tools, cutting boards, apron and wipe cloths are covered with bacteria.

Chapter 6 - Importance of Marketing

What is marketing

Marketing can be defined as a constant, ongoing effort to know and understand your trading area and your community so that you may take advantage of all opportunities to promote your business. Understanding who you are selling to and the market in which you are doing so creates lasting relationships and the need of the people in your area.

Marketing plays a huge role in the success of your company whether you are a distributor or restaurant owner. How you portray your company or products can make or break your success.

The components of marketing are really simple. However, all the new social media venues, added to the already existing choices, make the subject seem really complicated.

Let's boil it down to the lowest common denominator. The purpose of marketing is to let potential customers know, and remind existing customers, three things:

1. Who you are.

2. What you do.

3. Where you are located.

As a business owner, your marketing plan should include letting everyone in your marketing area know and remember those three things.

Right now, at this very minute, there are people in need of your products and services. However, these potential customers are going to your competitor because they know who your competitor is, what your competitor does and how to find them.

If people who don't need your products or services at this very moment happen to hear or read your advertising but may need them in the next day or next week, you are "branding" for future business.

The reason most people think it doesn't work is because when they spend money on a radio station advertisement, newspaper, website, yellow pages or billboards, there doesn't seem to be an immediate surge in business.

Think of it as "word of mouth" marketing and branding. Only you are in control of the words you are using and the message you want to get across. Relying solely on someone else's words may not tell the story exactly like you want it told. Besides, there will always be someone who will talk about your store or restaurant in a negative way, and you want to have plenty of positive exposures to offset those unfortunate situations.

For example: "My name is Joe Smith, owner of your local neighborhood IGA Grocery Store."

"Our highly skilled and knowledgeable meat cutters will show you on how to amaze your friends and family when they eagerly show you how to prepare and serve meals that will really be impressive. We also have a huge selection of locally grown produce, as well as a deli department with a unique selection of meats and cheeses that you'll find nowhere else. One visit is all it takes to see why so many loyal customers rave about our store."

"We are located in Edmond on the SE corner of Western Ave and Memorial Road with plenty of parking."

Notice on the "what you do" example of the marketing example I have incorporated an ID, which means an Identifiable Difference. It is imperative that you avoid overworked clichés such as: best service in town, the best kept secret in town, we're slashing prices to the bone.

These overused phrases are like trying to sell a piece of white paper by holding it up to a white background. Using a well thought out ID will be like selling a white piece of paper using a black background. An ID will make you stand out and be noticed, which is really important, here's why.

Back in the 1980s and early 1990s, it was understood that if someone saw or heard your marketing message 2 or 3 times, it would be remembered. Today it has jumped to between 6 and 8 times to be remembered. The amount of advertising messages each person receives on a daily basis has grown considerably. To be remembered, it has to stand out with an ID.

If you were to put a similar short and precise message on the local radio station (recorded by you), in the local newspaper (with your picture), on the local television station (with you doing the commercial), on all your social media networks, in the yellow pages, on a targeted postcard mailing to all the neighborhoods surrounding your store or restaurant, what do you think would happen? Would it work?

I can predict with 100% certainty that it would work IF it was done consistently and you lived up to your promise of: A meat department staff that "eagerly" showed customers how to prepare amazing meals and you DO carry a huge selection of locally grown produce.

The biggest mistake in marketing is relying on an advertising sales person to design your ad or hiring an agency to write your sales copy. No one knows your business like YOU do.

All you have to do is answer the above three questions and make sure you include an ID - IDENTIFIABLE DIFFERENCE-THAT YOU CONSISTENTLY LIVE UP TO.

You are your message

The single most important aspect of marketing your business or products is that you are selling yourself. When being yourself and making the customer feel as if they would be missing out if they didn't come to your business or buy your products, it is hard not to get the sale or the success that you should.

Promote who you are and what you are trying to accomplish and have your entire staff buy in to the ideas that you are portraying. If everyone is on board with those ideas, when people visit your company or your team is out in the field, it is very difficult to not have people jump on board just by the vibes that you are making them feel. They almost always feel like "Why haven't I bought from them" or "Those people just have it going on."

Talking with people, finding out their needs, creating relationships, understanding personalities should always be top priority before trying to sell something.

Inside sales

You can no longer depend solely on the quality of your food, the cleanliness of your restaurant or your excellent location to keep loyal customers returning. In today's competitive market you must actively and continually communicate to your customers and your employees how important they are to your success.

Your present customers are your greatest opportunity for increased sales because they are already predisposed to like and react positively to information concerning new menu items, extended hours or party catering suggestions.

A major part of in-store marketing is motivating your employees and providing them with incentives for doing the best job they can. Well-trained and highly motivated employees are an essential key to the success of your marketing plan.

You should involve your employees in every aspect of your marketing efforts. Asking them for their input and their ideas and rewarding them for their performance can be the difference between success and failure.

Too often, restaurateurs' resort to using the same old table tents, place mats or menu add-on pieces over and over again with the same offers or discounts. Just as you, as a customer, would finally ignore or overlook signs which were never changed or moved at your local grocery store, so do your customers begin to ignore your advertising when it always appears to be the same thing time after time.

There are numerous ideas you can develop inexpensively for communicating with your customers if you use your imagination.

If you have a place mat or tray liner program, have them printed with just your logo and perhaps a border. Each week you can develop a new message that you can have overprinted on the blank mats at your local quick-print shop.

These can be used to introduce new menu items or specials, but don't overlook the chance to use them to tell your customers about your involvement in their community.

As an example, announce upcoming special events in your community or give a free advertisement to the school carnival, the Girl Scout cookie sales, or the American Cancer Society's walk-a-thon. Make sure the group knows how nice you are to help them out!

If you see a good article in the newspaper or elsewhere about fire safety, poison treatment or other home safety tips, get permission to reprint it and use that as a place mat it could end up posted on the customer's refrigerator - along with your logo!

If you use blackboards to announce specials, make them work. Announce your involvement in a fundraiser to buy new band uniforms for the high school. Tie your donation to the check average of your customers and promote wine, desserts or higher priced menu items on your blackboard along with the fundraiser announcement.

Perhaps you can create a Special Reservations card with a private line phone number for your very special customers. Or present all your customers with a cross promotion coupon good for a 15% discount at the nearby record store, a "free rose with any purchase" for the florist next door or a free wax at the car wash around the corner.

Don't forget special decor and signage to expand the underline any major promotion or advertising campaign you run in outside media. For every media or advertising campaign you run on the outside, follow through with the same theme throughout your restaurant.

If you are running ads about your new "Chef's Specials'... follow through! Have your waitstaff wear chef's hats. Place chef's hat table tents throughout the restaurant. Check your specialty advertising suppliers for items like this. Bring your chef out of the kitchen. Have him or her walk around two or three times during the evening to introduce himself or herself.

Give every customer a bounce-back coupon valid for a discount the next time they order one of the Chef's Specials. Try a sampling event each evening to introduce your customers to a different Chef's Special.

The idea is to make everything you do into a "complete" promotion. Think how you can expand a promotion to include all aspects of marketing. See if you can get your chef on the local cooking show or offer one of his recipes to the food editor of the newspaper. You might invite a local charity to hold a one-night fundraiser with a portion of all sales on Chef's Specials going to the charity.

The result will be loyal customers and increased sales.

Chapter 7 - Menu Strategies

The menu is the most important sales tool a restaurant has and it must look attractive to people who are looking at it.

Explain complicated names

If you have featured dishes with a name that some people aren't familiar with, you should give a brief description of what it is so that you can get your customer to be attracted to it.

Tell your story

Use your menu to tell your story and let it reflect who you are and what you have to offer.

Keep your menu interesting

When changing your menu and adding new items, you should always try and keep 60% of the menu the same, while changing just 40%.

All you can eat buffet

Food costs are a huge concern for a buffet. Many folks who eat at a buffet are heavy eaters and makes it difficult to reach a desired food cost. Food cost at an all you can eat buffet can run as high as fifty and sixty percent. Portion control is also very difficult to manage, however, here are a few strategies to help keep it profitable:

- The fewer meat items, the better

- Heavy breaded items help fill people up

- Salads and soups are also a great way to fill customers up and keep food cots down

Keep your menu focused

A focused menu is one of the ways to be successful in the restaurant business. When you have a focused menu, it means you have multiple menu items from single inventory item. You are using the product in several different applications. This can help you expand your menu without having to add too much more inventory. Planning your menu whose ingredients can be used in more than one way.

Menu pricing

Pricing the menu can be done in a couple different ways. **The factoring method** is done by multiplying the cost of ingredients by three or four.
The gross margin pricing is a method used when the cost of ingredients is high.
The prime cost method is done by adding the cost of labor and the cost of food, then add a percentage for profit.

The combination pricing is a method which involves a little from each different approach. You must consider factoring, gross profit, prime cost, and competition approaches for different dishes.

The competition pricing method involves taking competitive information from your marketing area and compares it with similar items on your menu.

Price as a marketing tool. Understanding that by lowering your price of your products may add more sales, then sometimes you can add to the gross profit and increase sales just by lowering your price.

Profit is key. But all methods relate to a common denominator. The bottom line is not exactly how to determine your price, but how much money you make!

Importance of preparation time

Every great restaurant must set a time limit of 10 minutes for food preparation. This means tailoring your menu with items that this can be accomplished. If a meal is going to take longer than 10 minutes to prepare, your customer must be warned.

Chapter 8 - Staff Motivation

Most positions in the service industry are very important in making or breaking your company as well as the business model you are trying to portray. Each position inside the company has a specific role and the greatest asset that any company can have is the actual managers and employees. Increasing the productivity of your staff is one of the smartest business management practices.

There are nine factors that are considered when looking for the "perfect job":
1. Security
2. Opportunity
3. Training
4. Respect
5. Challenge
6. Growth
7. Pride
8. Expectations
9. Recognition

The most important, and most ignored, are expectations and recognition.

Expectations

Expectations will create a great attitude and an environment that is unmatched. An example of expectations for a wait staff person include: being on time, customer service, details, attitude, and job knowledge. A wait staff person should know these 5 expectations should consistently be met.

Recognition and appreciation

One of the most effective ways of keeping an employee interested in their job is by taking interest in them and make them feel appreciated. This can create a work ethic that every workplace is searching for.

Recognition has to be measurable so we can create a program that is tailored around something you would like to see them accomplish. Praise and recognition can help an employee achieve more and be more productive throughout their day. There is a huge cost for unproductive employees so keeping them motivated is very important.

Creating programs that are **specific and measurable** is the key to being successful. Programs must also be ongoing as well as something that can go in an employee's file for future references. However, there are some programs that work and then there are some that do not work.

Programs that do not work are things like employee of the month, employee of the quarter, parking spot, and time on the job. The better programs are the ones where the performance is tied into the 5 expectations of the employer. Many companies create promotions for certain achievements, and this will be something that is measurable and keep the employee motivated. If you tie in a recognition program with each of the five job expectations that you put together, it will pay continuous dividends.

Chapter 9 - What Makes A good steak

Breed: 10% of the quality

There are over 70 breeds of cattle in the U.S. Many of them have been cross bred resulting in a cattle population of between 125 and 150 million head of "Generic "cattle.

Regardless of whether it is a Hereford, Angus or "Generic", the breed alone does not guarantee the meat will have a good flavor and tenderness.

All cattle must be grain fed and meet the USDA grading requirements of choice or higher to result in a high-quality Ribeye, NY Strip, Tenderloin, etc.

Aging: 45% of the quality

What happens during the aging process is the connective tissue, a small fiber connecting the cells, breaks down and makes the meat less tough. It takes between 14 and 21 days for this break down to occur depending on the age and texture of the meat.

Without any aging the meat is extremely tough and has little flavor.

Percent of Improved Tenderness from aging:

6 days improves tenderness 50%

12 days improves tenderness 62%

18 days improves tenderness 78%

24 days improves tenderness 88%

28 days small additional improvement

Grade: 45% of the quality

USDA Prime has the highest amount of marbling and is considered the best eating experience.

USDA Choice There are actually three levels of USDA CHOICE. Each level is determined by the amount of marbling. They are referred to as "high choice, middle choice, and low choice." Most of the meat sold is "low" choice. "Middle" and "high" choice are sold to the beef branded programs such as Sterling Silver, Certified Angus Beef, etc.

USDA SELECT has the least amount of marbling and if cut as a steak is usually tough unless it is somehow tenderized.

Unsatisfactory eating experiences determined by the Colorado State University Agriculture Department.

Prime   1 out of 18

Choice   1 out of 9

Select   1 out of 4

No roll   1 out of 2

"Beef Branded Program"

In the mid 1970's a huge change took place in the beef industry. The discovery of cholesterol made everyone aware of the fat and marbling in the meat they were buying at the supermarket. The USDA responded by changing the grading system which resulted in a much leaner beef. The problem was that the fat (marbling) in beef is one of the main ingredients that makes the meat taste good resulting in a sales decline.

This opened the door for an opportunity to create brand identity. Brand identity means they took a commodity product and by requiring certain standards and specifications ended up with a consistent high quality beef.

Estimating plate cost

This is a simple way to find your approximate plate cost. It includes an allowance for labor, shrink, waste, mis-cuts and possible theft.

A lip-on Ribeye: Double the boxed price per lb to find your plate cost.

A lip-on NY Strip: Double the boxed price per lb to find your plate cost.

A PSMO Tender: Double the boxed price per lb to find your plate cost.

Chapter 10 - Portion Cut Steaks

Advantages of portion cut steaks:

Portion control

When steaks are cut at a meat plant every time, they cut a steak they put it on a portion scale and put it in a box with the same size steaks. If they cut a 5 oz, 6 oz, 7 oz, 8 oz, they do not have to worry about it. They have a need for each size. In a small operation we may want only 8 oz steaks and it is nearly impossible to cut an exact size every cut.

Consistency

Our customers expect consistency in both portion size and quality. A meat portion cutting operation has much better buying power plus the ability to resell anything that does not meet their specifications. A restaurant has non of these options.

Inventory control

It is much easier with precut steaks as you always know how many steaks are on hand compared to how many have been sold.

Meat cutter

It is very difficult to find a good meat cutter for a foodservice operation and it is not cost effective to have the owner or manager cutting steaks instead of managing the business.

Proper aging

Proper aging is another factor. When steaks are cut at a meat plant they are aged for a specific period of time and then processed. In a restaurant, if the meat comes in on Friday and a steak is immediately cut and served it may only have a few days age resulting in a tough steak and an unsatisfied customer. A precut steak will solve this problem.

Food safety

Food safety is another factor. Ninety four percent of all the bacteria found in food comes from mis-handling raw meat.

Chapter 11 - Selling Ground Meats

Ground beef labels

Ground Sirloin Patty: Meat and fat must come from the sirloin. Maximum fat 30%.

Ground Round Patty: Meat and fat must come from the round. Maximum fat 30%

Ground Chuck Patty: Meat and fat must come from the chuck. Maximum fat 30%

Ground Beef Patty: Made from primal cuts and primal trimmings. Nothing else can be added. Maximum fat 30%.

Pure Beef Patty: Made from primal cuts, primal trimmings and other non-primal meats such as shank meat and kidney fat. Any amount of *PDCB may be added without being on the label. Maximum fat 30%

Chuck Wagon Patty: Can be made from nearly any kind of meat, however, it must be listed on the label.

*PDCB Partially Defatted Chopped Beef is a meat by-product derived from the low temperature (120 degrees or lower) rendering beef trimmings containing more than 12% lean meat. May be in pure beef patties without being on the label. Pure beef patties are the only product it can be added to without being on the label.

85/15 or 80/20

As simple as this question may sound, it is understandable why it is asked. When someone first enters the foodservice business, they have to learn a whole new language. It is like learning to operate a computer. You cannot just sit down at the keyboard and know what to do. Yet many salespeople are sent out on the street without the proper knowledge and expected to know the language. Our business is filled with abbreviations and terms that are impossible to know except by asking. I remember selling different sieve sizes on green beans for nearly a year before I finally found out what a sieve size was. The same with WOG chickens, BRT hams, P&D shrimp, TVP, PDBT, etc. The term 85/15 means 85 percent lean meat and 15 percent fat. 80/20 meats 80 percent lean meat and 20 percent fat. **The important point to remember is that it is OK to ask.**

Cooking temperature

Most bacteria are on the surface of the meat where the temperature reaches a safe level long before the internal temperature reaches an equally safe level. When ground meats are processed the surface bacteria can be ground and mixed throughout product. This is why it is important to cook ground products to an internal temperature of at least 155 degrees for patties with a preferable temperature of 165 degrees for meatloaf and other recipes using ground meats.

Bacteria growth in ground beef

When products are kept below 35 degrees bacterial growth will virtually stop. It is important to remember that most bacteria is not damaged or killed by freezing, they simply do not multiply. Bacteria will grow and multiply at temperatures between 40 degrees and 140 degrees with the most rapid growth in the temperature range of 80-100 degrees. Ground beef should be stored properly and cooked to an internal temperature of at least 155 degrees.

Gray or brown in the middle

When hamburger meat is ground at the grocery store, the blood in the meat is oxygenated and turns red. Over time the oxygen is lost, and the meat loses its "bloom". That happens quicker in the middle of the package, but it is still safe. Fresh ground meat should be used within one or two days.

Requirements for a beef patty

According to the USDA the only requirement for a patty is that it is in the shape of a patty. A patty mix is anything that can be made into the shape of a patty. The important thing to look for is what is in front of the word patty. For example, a ground beef patty is a product that has no more that 30% fat and is made from ground beef. On the other hand, a "chuck wagon" patty can be made from just about anything that can be shaped into a patty, however, the ingredients must be listed on the label.

Chapter 12 - Selling Fresh Pork

How the pork market works

The pork market is similar to a pipeline. If we have 240 million pounds going into the pipeline per week, that means 240 million pounds have to come out. Also keep in mind that we have whole hogs going in so we have to have whole hogs coming out. If, on one particular week, 50 million people decide not to eat their pound of pork, we will have 50 million pounds left in the pipeline. We still have the 240 million pounds going in, so the price on the new pork will have to be lowered to be sure it will move through the pipeline.

The effect on price

The effect this has at a distributor level is that two salespeople selling the exact same ham from the same pork company could have two different prices. One could have inventory on hand at the old higher price and the other could have inventory at the new lower price. The market changes daily depending on the supply and demand.

There is a grading system for pork; however, it is only at the processing level. The whole hogs are graded as a

Number One, Number Two, Number Three, etc., each representing a different quality level. After the hogs are cut up and processed there is no grading system.

Reason for inconsistency

The reason you are having a problem with consistency is probably because of the method used for buying. Each processing plant has certain specifications for their fresh pork loins, pork butts, fresh hams, etc. When buying on price alone and continually switching from one packer to another to save a few pennies you end up with inconsistent quality due to the different quality specifications, what their advantages and disadvantages are, what different value added products are available such as special trim, boneless cuts, special packaging, and then to go out and build your fresh pork business the old fashioned way; by selling.

Fresh pork terms:

Pork butts... the top half of a pork shoulder...used mostly by Chinese and BBQ restaurants. .it is not recommended as a foodservice pork roast because of the fat...

Pork picnics the lower half of the pork shoulder...used very little in foodservice...sometimes processed as a slicing picnic used in place of a boiled ham...

Cushion... A lean piece of meat removed from the picnic.. used in any dish that requires lean pork...weighs about half a pound...

Pork collars... A two-inch piece of meat cut between the head and shoulder...most all pork collars are imported from Canada or Denmark... used in place of a pork butt...

Boneless pork loins... A loin with the back ribs, blade bone and hip bone removed...excellent for many foodservice uses...

B/l pork loins... A pork loin with all the bones left in weighing between 13 and 18 pounds...used in retail and foodservice for chops and roasts...

Canadian backs... The same as a boneless pork loin only trimmed closer with the ends squared...does not mean the product came from Canada...refers to how they trim them in Canada.

BRT pork roast... Means the meat was "boned, rolled and tied". Normally made from the hog's leg, however, it can be any piece of meat...

Pork tenderloin... A lean, tender piece of meat from the inside of the loin...comes in two sizes...1.5 lbs and up...1.5 lbs and down... high quality used for special recipes in white table cloth restaurant and country clubs...

Quarter loin pork chop... A quarter loin chop is a good marketing name for end cuts. To cut a package of quarter loin chops you would take a whole pork loin and cut 1/8" off each end making a quarter of the loin. Cutting it in this manner leaves the entire center of the loin for further merchandising at a higher margin, such as center cut pork chops or center cut pork roasts. Quarter loin chops are normally sold at a fairly low price making them a good value at the retail counter; however, they are very seldom sold in foodservice. When they are sold in foodservice, they are normally called rib end chops or loin end chops.

B/l chops… A bone in pork chop is cut from the loin...best quality is a center cut...when the end chops are left in it makes a very poor menu item...the end chops can be as much as 50% bone…

Boneless chops... A boneless pork chop is always best for foodservice, It can be prepared many different ways and has 100% yield…

America's cut... A center cut boneless pork chop at least 1 1/4" inches thick...introduced several years ago by the National Pork Council...

Spare ribs... The bones from the rib cage of the hog...different sizes available... most popular in foodservice is 3.5 dn.. meaning the whole rib weighs 3.5 lbs or less...

St Louis rib... A 3.5 down rib that has been trimmed. Sometimes called "trimmed rib".. the breast bone is removed making it easy to cut between the ribs..

Back ribs... The bones from a pork loin.. available in several sizes from a 1.2 dn to 2.5 lb.. a baby back rib refers to a rib weighing approximately 1.5 lbs or less..

Riblets... Small bones cut off the pork loin or the spare rib....when cut off the spare rib they are sometimes referred to as "bottom bones."

Prime Rib of Pork... Take the rib section (consisting of 11 ribs) out of a 14/17 pork loin, gently marinate it with approximately 12% of a lightly seasoned marinate to keep it moist, cut off the back bone so you can cut between the ribs, and you have a menu item that guarantees a great eating experience. When you slice between the ribs you have a portion size of 8 to 9 ounces at a cost of around $1.80. Add a potato, vegetable and salad for an additional $.50 cents and you have a total plate cost of only $2.30. Here's the best part: with a menu price of only $7.95 the food cost is less than 30% and the gross profit is $5.65 per plate. It gets better. Sell 200 per week (10,000 per year) for a total gross sales $79,500. Cost $23,000. Total Gross Profit $56,500. This is an example of the power of a carefully selected menu item that will give the restaurant customer a good value at gross profit that can really make a difference. Even with a dollar off special, it will still return a very nice gross profit.

Chapter 13 - Ham and Bacon

Categories determine the price.

Category one is called a "dry ham". This ham actually weighs less than it did when it was a raw fresh ham. Country hams are classified as dry hams. There are also some buffet hams that are considered dry hams.

Category two is ham with natural juice. This type of ham has the same moisture content as a raw fresh ham. No water has been added.

Category three is ham water added. A ham in the water added category has approximately 10% water added.

Category four is called a ham and water product. This is where the weight is more than 10% of the weight started with and the percent of water added must be stated on the label. There are hams with as much as 45% added ingredients. Added ingredients simply means water and spices.

Many meat products have water added to lower the cost. Every time we go to the sink, cut open a bag and pour off the water it is the same as throwing money away. If we were buying a ham, and after it set in the cooler for a few days noticed an excessive amount of water in the bag, it should be tested.

Ham terms:

Natural juice buffet ham - Highest quality ham...has no extra water added...usually made from inside muscles...should always be recommended first...

Water Added - Excellent quality ham...has approximately 10% water added...usually made from outside muscles...should be recommended second...

Ham and Water Product - This product has over 10% water added and the percent of added ingredient must be on the label...keep in mind that the more water that is added to the ham the less taste and flavor it will have...

Water and Ham Product - This is a new category designed for buyers who want an inexpensive low quality product...it is over half water and will have a very low flavor profile compared to a natural juice or water added ham.

Cooked 4x4 / 4x6 - Cooked means the product was not exposed to oven heat or smoke...it is sealed in a bag, put in a mold that gives it a size of 4 / 4 inches or 4 / 6 inches and then boiled...it is also referred to as a deli ham or a boiled ham... Primarily for making sandwiches.

Football - sometimes called a "bolo" ham...used when it is sliced in front of the customer...always check the label for the category and fat free statement.

Bone in - Has the center bone, aitch (hip) bone and shank bone left in, semi boneless has only the one center bone left in, usually in the water added category, mostly sold in retail.

Smoked pork loin - cured and smoked the same as a ham...must be labeled the same as a ham, pork loin water added or pork loin and water product 25% added ingredient...smoked pork chop makes an excellent menu item.

Honey cured ham - means the ham had honey used as part of the curing process...honey glazed means the ham was glazed on the outside only...must be in one of the categories: water added, ham and water etc.

Bacon

The size of the belly is the first factor. When the belly is first taken off the hog it is weighed and sorted out by size. The size ranges are 10/12, meaning the belly weighs between 10 and 12 pounds, 12/14, 14/16 and 16/18. The key to remember is the larger the belly the less expensive and lower quality it is.

The second factor is if the bacon is sliced end-to-end or if it is center cut. When we think about a center cut we normally think of it being the very center, however on bacon the center means the ends have been removed, about 5% off each end, leaving 90% of the belly.

Sliced slab is bacon that is still stacked together.

Layout bacon has been laid out flat on parchment paper and visually inspected for quality. The first person to see the sliced slab bacon is the person pulling it apart and putting it on the grill.

The next factor is the grade. There are only two grades of bacon, number one and number two. Number one bacon is within the manufacturer's specifications and number two is not. As the bacon is sliced and it is coming off the line there is a person inspecting the bacon. This person carefully checks the quality of the bacon to make sure it is within the specifications of the level of bacon they are running at the time. Any bacon that does not meet these specifications will be pulled off and put in a number two box.

When buying number two bacon the important thing to keep in mind is the lack of consistency in both quality and slice count. You may get some that looks real good and the next time it could look like it was all fat. Sliced slab still has the number two bacon mixed in and is less expensive.

Slice count

Another very important point is the desired thickness. Many operators are buying a large belly 14/18 slice count and think that if they used an 18/22 it would be too thin. By using a smaller belly and a higher slice count the bacon will still be thick, it will just be a little shorter. This one point can save an operator several thousand dollars.

Precooked bacon

The theory behind precooked bacon is, first of all, no grease. This saves on clean up as well as freight, keeping in mind that bacon is 50 to 60 percent fat. If an operator was using 75 pounds of bacon per week, that means that in the course of a year, there will be over one ton of grease that has to be removed. Another advantage is no broken slices, which saves on waste. Precooked bacon only takes one minute to cook, making it an excellent product for a sandwich shop as it can be put in a microwave.

Round Bacon

The theory of round bacon is that it gives better coverage on a round sandwich. Even though the round bacon is more per pound, it has a lower portion cost. Round bacon is made by rolling up the belly before it is smoked.

Canadian bacon

Canadian bacon is made by curing and smoking a "Canadian Back" which is actually a boneless pork loin that has been trimmed. In food service the biggest use for Canadian bacon is when preparing eggs Benedict. The largest problem an operator has is the amount of product they have to buy in order to have it available for a very slow-moving menu item. Many operators buy Canadian bacon at the supermarket where they can buy it in a small package.

Bacon terms:

Slice counts - 14/18, 18/22, 22/26 refers to the number of slices per pound...a 14/18 will have 240 slices in a 15-pound box and an 18/22 will have 300 slices per 15 pound box.

CC Layout - CC stands for center cut. Layout means the bacon is laid out flat on a parchment paper.

Sliced slab - means the bacon has been stacked together as it was sliced and remains in the shape of the slab...it costs between $.15 and $.20 cents per pound to separate sliced slab and put it on the grill.

Number two - bacon that did not meet the specifications of the layout bacon that was being sliced. It is pulled off the slicing line, put in number two box and sold at a discount.

Market style - usually made from a large belly. Sliced end to end (it is not a center cut) ...and thick sliced...usually 14/18. It is sold in bulk at meat markets and supermarkets. It is not recommended for foodservice however, because of the low price it is sometimes requested.

Chapter 14 - Poultry Products

Approximately 75% of all chicken sold to food service operators is frozen or further processed.

Handle with care

One of the down sides in using fresh chicken is bacteria that comes from the intestines of a chicken. This bacteria causes salmonella poisoning. The symptoms are the same as a bad case of flu. The bacteria is present in about one third of the fresh chickens and the bacteria is normally spread by improper handling of the chicken.

If a fresh chicken is cut up and the cutting board is not cleaned before reusing, the bacteria can spread. Salmonella is killed by heat. It takes 60 seconds to kill the bacteria at 145 degrees, 6 seconds at 155 degrees and only 1 second at 165 degrees.

Chicken tender

A "chicken tender" is simply a tender piece of chicken. It can be made from any piece of young chicken. The key to look for is if it is a chicken "tender" or a chicken "tenderloin." A chicken tenderloin is a specific piece of meat located near the breast bone underneath the breast meat. It is a very high-quality piece of meat and makes an excellent menu item when breaded and fried.

How much "marinate" can be added to a chicken breast before it affects the quality or price?

Meat products containing 10% or less marinate will have a label that will state that the product is marinated, however, once the amount of marinate exceeds 10% it must be on the label.

Free range chicken

In 1935 it took five pounds of feed for every one pound of chicken and 16 to 17 weeks to raise a three-pound chicken. Today it only takes approximately 1.9 lbs. of feed for each pound of chicken and only 6 to 7 weeks to grow to three pounds.

They still raise the chickens that take 16 to 17 weeks, they are called "free range chickens". These chickens are raised without the aid of feed additives that make them grow at a faster rate.

Cooking chicken

Chicken should be cooked so the internal temperature is 160 degrees. The recommended internal temperature by the USDA is 145 degrees, however, a slightly higher temperature on chicken actually softens the proteins making it tender.

Dark meat and white meat

Meat is muscle and muscle that is active stores a lot of oxygen from the blood. This makes the meat darker than meat from muscles that are less used. Chickens walk but do not fly resulting in leg and thigh meat that is dark and breast and wing meat that is white. White meat always brings more money, so by growing an all-white chicken we could make more money.

Yellow and white chickens

The color of the chicken is determined by the type of feed it is given. In retail a yellow chicken has a very attractive eye appeal compared to a pale looking white chicken. In foodservice the white skin is actually more desirable. It has been my experience that yellow chicken has more oil in the skin and when deep frying a breaded product the breading has a tendency to pop off.

Further processed turkey

Turkey is available in several further processed items. When the turkey is separated into the different cuts, each part has a different use.

The tails have little value and are shipped to other countries. For example, Mexico uses them to make taco meat.

The wings are deboned and used for ground white meat in the supermarket.

The drumsticks are used for foodservice ground turkey.

The thighs are used to make the turkey lunch meat items such as hams, pastrami, bologna, hot dogs, etc. and the backs are mechanically deboned and used as filler in some of the lunch meats.

Turkey lunch meats

Processed turkey lunch meats can represent a tremendous savings if they can replace the higher priced beef and pork lunch meats. If you are looking for inexpensive items to use on a sandwich buffet or some low-price hot dogs, turkey might well fill the need.

Turkey breast

If the turkey breast is **oven roasted** it will be more expensive than a breast that was **oven prepared**. However, today the two terms have the same meaning.

A product that is hand formed, meaning that a person actually places the turkey breast in the mold, will be more expensive than one that is machine stuffed.

The number of major muscles will have a definite effect on the price. A breast with two to three breast pieces will be more expensive than a breast with four to five pieces. A breast with seven to eight pieces will be more expensive than a breast made from multiple pieces (more than eight). The number of pieces can be identified when the breast is sliced.

Turkey tenderloin

If the tenderloin is left in, the price will be lower. A turkey tenderloin located near the breast bone, the same as on a chicken, has a piece of gristle going through the center and makes it undesirable. When the turkey breast is sliced the tenderloin can be identified and you can easily spot both the tenderloin and the piece of gristle. The tenderloin, by itself, can be made into some very nice products.

If the skin is left on, the price will be lower than if the skin was removed. The natural proportion is 15%. If the skin is on, it may have been "defatted", meaning that the skin was removed, the fat was scraped off and the skin is then placed back on the breast. This is called the "toupee" method.

Chapter 15 - Specialty Meats

Quail:

Quail is an extremely lean product and considered one of the most popular game birds. They are farm raised and take about six weeks to grow large enough to yield about 6 ounces dressed weight. Quail makes an excellent menu addition for many different segments such as steak houses, seafood restaurants, hotel restaurants and can also be found in hospitals and nursing homes.

Foie Gras:

Foie Gras is a French term that means "fat liver" and is used to denote a class of products derived from duck and goose. Foie Gras is made from duck and goose livers that, through a special feeding process, have been fattened, giving them a very rich flavor. It is mixed with some other products and made into a pate, served at some of the more expensive restaurants.

Alligator:

There are about 150 alligator farms in Florida and Louisiana with more than 75,000 alligators in captivity. About 35,000 alligators are harvested each year for processing and distribution. The alligator normally lays about 38 eggs in early summer resulting in tens of thousands of eggs that can be collected for hatching. Alligator farmers are learning how to produce and raise alligators in captivity for the market. They can now raise alligators 5 to 6 feet in less than three years.

Lamb:

When American lamb is compared to imported, it can be slightly more expensive. However, it is also a different product. Imported lamb comes from a smaller breed of sheep and is usually grass fed. If you are accustomed to the flavor of grain fed beef and pork, then you will appreciate the larger, meatier cuts and milder flavor of American lamb.

American lamb is also graded by the USDA. Maturity, color, firmness and texture of the lean are evaluated in terms of their relationship to the ultimate flavor and tenderness of the meat. Conformation is the term used to evaluate the carcass' general shape, form and outline. USDA lamb grades are Prime, Choice, Good, Utility and Cull. Almost all lamb sold in foodservice is graded Choice or Prime.

Common lamb terms:

BLOCK READY is lamb that is closely trimmed to specifications. The product may require cutting into portions prior to being used.

BRT meats boned, rolled and tied. A leg or shoulder that is completely boned, internal fat removed, and excessive outer fat trimmed off. When properly rolled it is ideal for a rotisserie or as an oven roast.

BUTTERFLIED LEG OF LAMB is a leg completely boned and "defatted" and used when the product is going to be cooked on a grill or broiled.

CROWN ROAST is made by curving around two rib halves, 8 ribs each and tying them to resemble a crown.

FRENCHING is the removal of, at least, one and a half inches of meat from the bone ends of a rib roast or rib chops.

GENUINE SPRING LAMB is meat labeled "genuine" lamb or simply "lamb" comes from an animal less than 1 year old. This is specified by the USDA regulations. Spring lamb identifies lamb processed between the first Monday in March through the first Monday in October. Years ago, lamb production peaked in spring and at other time customers may have been limited to frozen lamb. Now production is spread over 12 months and the "spring lamb" identity has lost its importance.

HIND SADDLE consists of both hind legs still connected, plus the sirloin, loin and flank.

MUTTON is meat from an animal that is over two years old.

The most versatile cut of lamb and veal to be put on the menu, but not being sure how it was going to sell, we would want to use the principle of multiple menu items from a single inventory product.

There is one cut of lamb that can be used to make at least eight menu items this item is a boneless sirloin butt. We could slice it and call it grilled sirloin lamb steak, we could cube it and call it lamb kabobs, we could cut it in thin slices for a lamb salad, we could make lamb fajitas, lamb stir fry, we could roast it in the oven and call it roast leg of lamb, we could make lamb stew and we could also make boneless sirloin lamb chops, all from a single piece of meat.

The same could be done on veal. From a sirloin butt we could make grilled sirloin - veal steak - veal kabobs - veal stew - boneless sirloin veal chops. When an operator takes this approach, it gives the appearance of having a large selection but they do not have to have a large inventory to back it up. If some of the items do not sell very well, our meat item is still turning over with no worry about spoilage.

Veal:

The meat that comes from cattle under the age of 9 months is often described generically by the word "veal." However, within that age group there are three different classifications based on the age of the animal at the time it is butchered and the way it has been fed.

Bob Veal: The youngest type of veal is called "Bob Veal." They are butchered at a weight of 150 pounds. The meat on these young animals is very light in color and has very little taste and texture. Bob veal is mostly fabricated into cutlets, cubed for stew, processed into veal patties, or breaded cutlets.

Special fed veal. The next classification is called "special fed veal." The animal is butchered between 350 and 400 pounds. Special fed veal is raised on a nutritionally complete diet resulting in meat that is firm, smooth, velvety texture and the traditional veal color, light pink. Special fed veal is mostly used for steaks, chops, roasts, and cutlets.

Calf veal. The third classification is called "calf veal." Calf veal is butchered between 5 and 9 months of age and weighs between 400 to 750 pounds. Their diet is different than special fed veal, usually including grain and hay. Because of a calf's age and diet, the meat varies greatly from the meat of special fed veal. Calf meat tends to be a deeper red, and some additional marbling and external fat may be present. If you are in any doubt about whether a piece of meat is calf or special fed veal, check the color. Calf is deeper red than the light pink of special fed. Most veal is graded USDA Prime or USDA Choice.

Chapter 16 - Seafood

The top ten terms to be aware of in the seafood industry:

Aquaculture - Oysters, salmon, trout, catfish, shrimp, redfish, striped bass, and tilapia are all being farmed. Provides a reliable consistent supply. Fish farming is still expensive, however, 12% of all US consumption is farmed raised.

Parasites – Parasites found in seafood, mostly in the form of worms. They are most common in tuna, salmon, drum, cod, and swordfish. They are easily removed with a knife. To reveal the parasites a process called candling is used. This is where the fillet is put on a cutting board with a bright light shining up from underneath exposing any parasites. Freezing and cooking kills the parasites, however, it is more desirable to have them removed rather than cooking and eating them. Caution should be used in any fish that is consumed raw.

Belly Burn – Belly Burn defect on dressed fish is caused by leaving the entrails in fish too long. A heat is created and deteriorates the cavity wall. A valid reason for rejecting fish. Found often in salmon.

When a fish is first caught it is very important that the intestines are removed as soon as possible. If the entrails are left in too long a bacterium begins to grow and when the fish is finally eviscerated there will be brown spot in the cavity. This spot is referred to as "belly burn" and results in an inferior product. It happens frequently in salmon and it is a legitimate reason for rejecting an order.

Clumping - Contents of a pack stuck together caused when product warms during shipment. Texture will be inferior

Dips – Dips are chemicals used to retain moisture. The most common is sodium tripolyphosphate. If this chemical is used it should be listed on the label and if it is not it is illegal. Tripolyphosphate reduces the gaping of fillets and keeps items like scallops and fillets from shrinking. If this chemical is used in excessive concentration the product becomes tough and hard to cook.

There are "dips" used in processing seafood which means the product is "dipped" in a solution of chemicals used to retain moisture. The most common is sodium tri-poly phosphate. This is in a salt form and when mixed in water it can be used to add water to seafood items. A certain amount of sodium tri-poly phosphate is useful as it keeps the product from losing moisture too fast. Scallops are a good example. You can almost watch them disappear. A small amount of sodium tri-poly phosphate can help retain moisture, prevent gaping and have a longer shelf life.

However, if it is used in excessive concentration the product becomes tough and hard to cook.

Gaping - is a term used to describe the separation of fish fillets. The fillet actually flakes apart. These flakes, as they are called, are joined by a connective tissue. When the fish first dies it is important not to handle the fish while it is going through a period of "rigor." During this period the fish stiffens and if it is handled these connective tissues will break apart.

Glaze - is a protective coating of water that is applied to the fillet after they are frozen. The product passes through a tunnel where a spray or mist is applied. This glaze is part of the packaging and not part of the net weight. It should never exceed more than .03% of the weight. If you see product with excessive glaze it is a signal to investigate further.

Ratpaking - is a term that means putting good product on the top of the box with lesser quality product in the lower half of the box. When the box is first opened and inspected it looks good, however, after they work their way down to the bottom of the box the quality also goes down.

Mushy Fillets - The ideal storage temperature for seafood is 20 degrees below zero. Even if the temperature fluctuates between 20 below and zero there will still be damage done to the product. This slight flexing of the cell wall will make the fillet mushy. Most of the damage is done during shipping or if the product is located near a freezer door that is frequently opened and closed, allowing the temperature to go up and down. Signs of temperature fluctuations are ice crystals, distorted shape, clumping and discoloration.

Breading - There is no more than 50% breading allowed on all seafood with the exception of USDC grade A and "lightly dusted," which may have no more than 30%.

The amount of breading allowed on seafood is different than what is allowed on meat patties. Meat patties such as breaded hamburger, pork, chicken, etc., are allowed to be no more than 30 percent breading. On seafood the amount of breading is 50 percent. If you were going to test the difference between two breaded products an easy way is to take a pound of each product being tested, making sure it is frozen, and wash the breading off using cold running water, then weigh the two products to see if they each weigh one half pound. This is also a good way to compare breaded shrimp.

There are thousands of species of fish and shellfish, however, the top ten make up over 80% of all the seafood consumed in the United States.

Top ten species

1. Tuna:

How can you do a pressed weight test on canned tuna?
Tuna has a pressed weight of 38 ounces for chunk and 43
ounces for solid. A method of checking and comparing the
pressed weight is to open both ends of the can, put it in the
sink and apply equal pressure to the two cans being
compared. After the oil or water has drained off, take the
product out of the container and check the weight to see if
they meet the minimum standard weight and how they
compare with each other.

2. Shrimp:

What are the three different grades of shrimp? Shrimp
is graded as A, B, or substandard. The grade is
determined by the amount of dehydration, deterioration,
pieces, size, unclean ends, texture and the presence of
legs, flippers and shells.

3. Cod

What does the term scrod refer to? Scrod is not a
species of fish but a marketing term. Any small fish can be
called a scrod.

4. Pollock

What fish is surimi made from? Surimi is a product made primarily from pollock, which is turned into a jello or paste like substance used as the main ingredient in imitation crab as well as other seafood items.

5. Salmon

What has more value a troll or net caught salmon? Troll caught salmon from the ocean is superior quality ... same fish caught 100 miles upriver before spawning would be pale, watery, almost inedible.

6. Catfish

What cost more a shank or regular fillet? A shank fillet is more expensive as the slightly lower quality nugget has been removed.

7. Clams

What is the difference between a sea and ocean clam? Sea clams are the highest quality clams. They are harvested in shallow water about 60 to 120 feet and take about 5 to 7 years to mature. Ocean clams are lower quality and have a tough texture. They are usually cut into a product called clam strips. Ocean clams are harvested in deeper water, 120 to 240 feet, and take 25 to 30 years to mature.

8. Flounder/sole

Is flounder a flat fish or a round fish? Flounder/sole are the name given to the most U.S. flat fish. The term flat fish describes a species that is born swimming upright and as it matures it rolls over on its side.

9. Scallops

What is a "25% water added scallop product?" The Government has attempted to regulate the scallop industry by sanctioning a wide-spread "sodium tri-poly phosphate soaking" process by requiring processors label the frozen scallops "Scallop Product 25% Water Added."

10. Crabmeat

What crab is used for "cocktail claws?" Stone crab is used for cocktail claws. When fishermen bring in the stone crab they twist off one claw and throw the crab back in the water. The crab grows another claw and if it is caught a second time the new claw is called a retread.

Buying seafood

The first and most important thing is to be sure you know who you are buying your seafood from. Buy products only from approved, reputable licensed stores, markets or distributors with evidence of good refrigeration, icing and sanitation.

Low price. Keep in mind that when someone is offering a really low price on an item there is usually a reason and a problem with why it is so cheap.

Fresh fish should have a mild sea breeze odor. A strong, fishy odor generally is not acceptable and means the quality of the fish is bad.

Whole fresh fish should have bright, clear and shiny eyes. Scales should be shiny and cling tightly to the skin and the gills should be bright pink or red.

Fresh steaks and fillets should be moist and free of drying or browning around the edges.

Frozen fish should be received in undamaged boxes and must be frozen solidly with no evidence of freezer burn.

Fresh "shell on" products such as mussels, clams and oysters should be purchased alive.

Live crabs will show leg movement and lobsters will curl their tails tightly beneath them when handled.

Freshly shucked oysters and scallops have a fresh odor and should be surrounded with a clear, slightly milky or light gray liquid. If in doubt about the source of raw oysters, clams and mussels, ask your supplier to show you the certified shipper's tag that must accompany shell on products.

Frozen shellfish should always be received in vacuum packed moisture proof containers.

Thawing seafood. Seafood should be thawed in the refrigerator or under cold running water. Do not thaw frozen seafood at room temperature or under warm running water. The outer edges can start to spoil before the center has thawed.

Chapter 17 Sustainability

Sustainable seafood is seafood that is either caught or farmed in ways that consider the long-term vitality of harvested species and the well-being of the oceans, as well as the livelihoods of fisheries-dependent communities. Being sustainable means that it is fished or farmed in a way that helps sustain wild, diverse, and healthy ecosystems.

Sustainable seafood movement:

Sustainability was first promoted through the sustainable seafood movement which began in the 1990s. This operation highlights overfishing and environmentally destructive fishing methods. Through a number of initiatives, the movement has increased awareness and raised concerns over the way our seafood is obtained.

Overfishing

Catching fish faster than they can reproduce is an urgent issue and is one of the biggest threats to ocean ecosystems. Today, roughly one-third of assessed fish populations are over-fished. Many fisheries around the world throw away more fish than they keep, and this is especially seen in the shrimp fisheries.

Bycatch:

In the worst cases, for every pound of shrimp caught, up to six pounds of other species are discarded and this incidental catch of unwanted or unsellable species, known as "bycatch." Sometimes this bycatch is fish too small to sell, other times it consists of animals such as sea turtles, dolphins, sea birds, and even whales that just get discarded.

Type of gear:

The types of gear used for fishing (both recreationally and commercially) also play a huge role in Sustainability. Gears that drag across the seafloor, like trawls and dredges, can destroy delicate habitats that provide shelter, food and breeding grounds for fish and other species. In heavily trawled areas, it's the equivalent of clear-cutting a forest. Among different fishing gear, bottom trawling and dredging are top offenders. Traps and pots cause less seafloor damage and catch fewer non-targeted species than other types of fishing gear that contact the seafloor.

Seafood Labels:

The Marine Stewardship Council (MSC) is a private organization that has a set of criteria intended to evaluate whether a wild fishery is sustainably managed. Seafood from fisheries that meet the criteria can receive MSC certification and bear a blue logo on their product label. MSC is a private certification, however, so it decides what standards a fishery must meet to qualify as sustainable under its own label. Unfortunately, not all of the fisheries that have received MSC certification are actually sustainably managed, which makes the MSC label confusing and not the best guide to seafood for consumers.

Aquaculture:

The Aquaculture Stewardship Council (ASC) is a newer entity (established 2009) related to and similar to the MSC in practice. It certifies only farm-raised seafood as "sustainable" if it meets certain criteria that the ASC establishes. Like MSC, ASC is a private entity that creates its own standards for what "sustainable" means. The ASC forms its standards based on "dialogues" - essentially group discussions with industry and some others. Also, like the MSC, the fish that ASC labels as sustainable is not always actually sustainably farmed, which also makes the ASC label confusing and not an ideal way for consumers to select sustainably farmed seafood.

Chapter 18 Where to find prospects

Current Customers

They are not only a source of reorders, but they are also prospects for product that you are not currently selling to them. Current customers are the best customers since they are already sold on you and the services marketed by your company, they are easier to sell new items to than trying to generate new sales through new customers. Current Customers also know their competitors. Don't be afraid to ask them for leads on new customers. DON'T talk too much, the sign of a great salesperson is to ask questions and get the customer talking as much as possible.

Online search

There are a large number of headings here which list your potential customers. Check both the yellow and white pages. Searching for topics/headings that are consistent with the type of business you are in and the type of customers you are looking for.

Newspapers/online reviews

Look for possible prospects in newspapers advertisements, restaurant reviews, or feature stories in your local newspapers and/or local online outlets. Don't overlook weekly food sections. Newspapers can also give you leads on new buildings being constructed and on renovations.

Local government offices

You can get information on construction permit, new businesses, and liquor licenses at local government offices.

City/membership directories

At many local public libraries, or at the Chamber of Commerce, you can obtain city directories of foodservice establishments. This can give you a great idea of all the foodservice establishments in the area of which you are trying to market.

Other distributor's salespeople

Some salespeople who call on foodservice establishments do not compete with you directly. They might include the route driver or sales rep for products such as ice cream, snacks, bread, liquor, soft drinks, perishables, uniforms and linens, and beer and wine. All you need to is ask them for information. Industry contacts like these are certainly one of your best sources of reliable information because we are all in the business together, and they are always willing to help people in the same industry if they are not directly your competition.

Membership in associations

Participate in local food related trade associations can help you learn a great deal about the foodservice industry in your area.

Territory surveillance

Research and contact can't be the only information you rely on. Business and foodservice establishments are always on the rise and popping up all over. Keeping your eyes open while on calls in your territory will help on getting new leads. If you see a new building going up, stop in and ask questions. Most of the time the early bird gets the worm, and in these situations it is no different. Take the long way when you are out in the field and be on the constant lookout.

Former customers

Keep in mind that turnover in the foodservice business is constant. They may be your customers now, but tomorrow, there may be a new manager, or your competitor may have messed up the account. By surveying former customers, you will know what is happening in your area, and by keeping relationships good and constant, former customers become current customers in the blink of an eye.

Social media

In today's economy, social media is a very important tool to use to prospect potential customers. The great thing about social networks is it is a constant demand for new content leads. Employees post all kinds of inside knowledge about the company they are working for. Choose a target company and research it. Search their posts for information on promotions, purchases, acquisitions and contracts. Once you have a clear idea of what they need, it is far easier to position yourself as the best solution.

Drivers

Your drivers are your marketing resources. Sometimes your customer sees your driver the most and he is a direct representation of your business. Keeping them running a tight ship and using them to be in the KNOW of what is going on in your market can help in establishing new and useful information. Get them asking questions and make sure they keep an eye out for things happening in your area. Use that information to capitalize on prospects.

This book is a summary of the complete course. For more information visit www.BobOros.com

www.ingramcontent.com/pod-product-compliance
Lightning Source LLC
Chambersburg PA
CBHW030805180526
45163CB00003B/1151